Empowering Change through Facilitation

Helping Others to Help Themselves

ISBN-13: 978-1523405640

First Published October 2008

ALA INTERNATIONAL PUBLISHING

Lutterworth, England - alapub@ala-international.com

Email - george.boulden@ala-international.com

Web site - www.ala-international.com

Ed 8 November 2016

Contents

Synopsis

The focal point of the Action learning philosophy is Revan's original idea that mature people learn best 'with and from each other'. In Action Learning programmes the learning opportunity is provided by a specific task, a project that each participant agrees with their 'client'. During the project participants meet every few weeks with a facilitator. The role of the facilitator is to 'manage the learning. In practice this means:

1. Developing understanding of and commitment to the Nature & Process of Change.
2. Encouraging participants to share their project experiences and reflect on the outcomes to identify their learning needs.
3. Working with participants using the KSEB methodology to converted learning needs into 'learning projects' thus linking reflection and learning.
4. Providing the environment in which participants are encouraged to achieve both their 'task and 'learning' goals.
5. Creating the conditions in which the set can become self-managing

Note. Whilst this book focuses on the Action Learning approach to Facilitated Learning all activities which have as their core purpose the goal of helping people to change their behaviour are facilitating learning.

Acknowledgements

I would like to begin by acknowledging the great debt of gratitude I owe to Professor Reginald (Reg) Revans, the founder of the Action Learning movement. We met in 1974 when he was planning his first Action Learning programme in GEC. At the time of our first meeting I had recently transferred from line management into a management development role. I was very aware that mature managers did not respond well to 'teaching' and was searching for ways of creating learning opportunities. Over lunch Reg shared his ideas with me and I was sold; thirty-five years later I am still a convinced action learner. He introduced me to Alan Lawlor who pioneered Own Job Action Learning in the West Midlands and the three of us created Action Learning Associates (ALA) Intentional in 1980 to promote the application of Action Learning. My relationship with Reg continued until his death in 2003.

I would also like to acknowledge my good friends Malcolm Farnsworth, John Cooper and Professor Steve Iman of Cal Poly Pomona CA.

Malcolm, who as Principal of the Marconi Staff Development Centre in Chelmsford, gave me the chance of a new career in management development which I have pursued for a very stimulating thirty-five years.

John, who I worked with at The Dunchurch College of Management, is a natural 'action learner' as anyone who has used or experienced the marvellous business simulations he created will testify and generous to a fault with everything he did. For me John is one of the unsung heroes of Action Learning and deserves to be recognised as such.

Steve for his encouragement and enormous contribution to the publication of the book; without Steve's guiding hand it would probably never have seen the light of day'

Finally I would like to thank the many hundreds of participants and clients from around the globe who I have learned with and from over the years. It has been a great privilege to know you, thank you all.

George P Boulden – January 2016

Facilitation Based Learning

The behaviour of individuals, organisations and societies, in any given situation, is determined by their individual values, portrayed in a style dictated by their cultural values and chosen by them as 'most appropriate' for the current situation (environment). Individual values determine '*what'* individuals, organisations and societies seek and seek to avoid: their personal goals. Cultural values determine '*how'* they do it - the way they go about trying to achieve their goals: their value relating style.

The person who likes to talk to strangers is motivated by an individual need to be involved with others. The procedure the individual uses to satisfy this need, making initial contact by saying 'Good morning' for example, is determined by what the individual believes is culturally appropriate in the circumstances. Once portrayed, the sender's behaviour is either reinforced or not, by the value systems of the other person.

If the response to the opening gambit is positive, it means that the other person accepts the opening remark, or is at least willing to be polite, and say's *Good morning to you...* as a culturally acceptable start for a conversation. If the response is negative the intervention has failed, either the recipient is not interested, or the approach is unacceptable. The start of the communication must be culturally and individually acceptable. Saying *Good morning*, or in the UK, *Terrible day again*, referring to the weather, are both acceptable start points for a discussion; trying to start the same conversation by stating your views on politics, religion or sex would normally be less successful.

Even if the need for contact is there and the 'style' of approach is acceptable the intervention may still fail for cultural reasons. If, for example, the first speaker is male and the person being addressed is a female who would like to talk, but has been brought up strictly not to talk with strangers; especially males.

Individuals, organisations and societies perception of the world is based on what they have learnt to believe during their formative years. Someone brought up to believe that they are 'superior' will naturally take a condescending attitude towards people who they see as 'inferior', even though they may be a caring person. Those who have been strongly conditioned in a particular belief system, religion for example, can readily reject other's beliefs without knowing anything about them. The historical view that men have rights and women have duties determines or determined role relationships. The male can't help assuming he is 'in charge' because the cultural values dictate this.

It is our personal values, seen through the eyes of our perception of our environment that determines our 'value relating style'. It is these 'relating behaviours' rather than individual needs or abilities, which I believe, have the most significant impact on individual, organisational and national performance. They create, and therefore are, the environment, in which people live and work. At 'work' the environment is created by the organisation, school, university or job, at home, by the family, at play by the social set and so on. The environment of organisations is made up of its markets, suppliers, competitors, trades unions etc., and the social values of the particular nation in which they operate - a factor that sometimes causes problems for multi-nationals operating in foreign lands. Societies are affected by the values of other societies. For example Japan's early success in achieving 'world class' levels of productivity was achieved largely due to a national commitment by its people to Japan Inc. The Japanese believe that what is good for Japan is good for them; in most Western nations however people believe in the principle of 'what's in it for me' making it more difficult to achieve the participative approach necessary to optimise productivity. Value systems are interlinked, one within the other. No individual, organisation or society ever acts totally independently; we are always influenced to some degree by others. It is our values Individual, organisational and cultural values that determine what we achieve.

See our book Change; Become a Winner available from Amazon.com for a more detailed explanation.

So, you may say, what does all this have to do with facilitation? The answer is everything. What we believe is what we are; our beliefs are based on our early experiences and these are handed down to us by our families and the societies in which we live. So our values are already dated when we form them. This means that in this fast changing world, whilst some of our values will be relevant to our current situation, others will be inappropriate and need to be changed.

It is the task of the facilitator to empower change which raises three questions:

1. Why do we need to be 'empowered to change?
2. What changes need facilitation?
3. How do we facilitate change?

Why do we need to be 'empowered' to change?

Because we can't just do it, our 'programming' won't allow us to. The quotation 'Give me a child until it's seven (years old) and I'll give you the man' from Richard Dawkins book 'The God Delusion' describes beautifully the power of human programming. It's very simple; we are encouraged in childhood, through a process of positive and negative reinforcement, to adopt a set of values. If we stay within the framework of what for us are OK (approved) beliefs and behaviours, we feel OK with ourselves and others who are doing the same. If we step outside our approved behaviour zone, we feel stress and we are not OK. So stress occurs naturally when we are in conflict with our values. Stress is the control, the governing force of behaviour and the further we go outside the guidelines the more stressful things become.

There are two types of stress, positive stress and negative stress. Positive stress occurs when we for example, stand up to make a formal presentation to our assembled bosses and peers. This is something we 'should' be able to do but is nonetheless stressful. However the stress is 'positive' because firstly it ensures that we will do the very best we can to make a good presentation and secondly when it's over the stress disappears. Negative stress occurs when we step outside the permissions of the programme to either do something we know that we are not supposed to do, like having one drink too many before driving home or when we are faced with doing something that we can do but don't want to do, like a boring repetitive job, or living with a relationship which we hate, or a boss who we really dislike. In the D&D example forgiveness is just around the corner, the stress will go away as soon as we are safely home and in the worst case, we lose our driving license for a few months. The real problem is the stress that is triggered by a job we don't like, a difficult relationship, a problem we can't solve; such situations will always be stressful unless we change something.

The task of the facilitator is to empower us to either change an existing behaviour or belief; something which is inappropriate to our current situation or to help us to embrace new behaviours or beliefs which need to be successful in today's world.

So what changes need facilitation?

Well it depends who you are facilitating. If it's an AA set, a STOP (smoking) set, a Weight Reduction set your task is to empower participants to stop doing something and through this enable them to create a new life for themselves. My main interest over the last forty years has been in management development looking at the behaviours that managers, brought up in Western cultures, need to change in order to be able to use a more participative style of management thus harnessing the brains and commitment of their people. Over the years we have conducted a study using Eric Berne's I'm OK Your OK model which clearly show that the traditional Western approach to management was (is?) predominantly Parent/Child.

Study of Management behaviours

Management Behaviours

| 2 | I'm Ok | 1 |

SUPPRESSED | ENCOURAGED

Asking questions	Making statements
Involving	Telling
Negotiating	Confronting
Planning	Action
Listening	Assuming
Leading	Following
Process	Task
Openness	Certainty
Thinking through	Doing it now
Proactive behaviour	Reactive behaviour
Innovation	Conformity

I'm Not Ok   You're Ok

| 4 | You're Not Ok | 3 |

Note: The above results have been observed in studies by us of over 500 managers in over ten different countries between 1985 and 1992.

The results indicate that many of the, what were at that time 'suppressed' behaviours, shown in quadrant 2, were we believe fundamental to the effective management of modern organisations. Particularly those concerned with such skills as negotiation, interviewing, performance review and counselling. Our role as was primarily to support the transfer of the required behaviours from 'suppressed' to 'encouraged'.

Note. Individual managers are not the real problem here; this I discovered very early in my work in management development lies in the organisation's values. Managers manage in the way they do because this is what the organisation's environment rewards. Thus, like Pavlov's dogs, people are 'moulded' into the shape of the organisations values. Those who do not like the mould are encouraged to leave.

How does the change process work?

There are three basic ways of bringing about change in individuals and organisations:

1. Natural Change - This is primarily an individually focused process. Expectations of change are programmed in the early years. They prepare us for the changes we can expect during our lives and give some basic understanding of how to handle them. For example, the individual expects to reach puberty, leave home, get married and have a family, grow old, and one day to die. Note. The expectation of the change does not necessarily reduce the trauma of the experience, but the knowledge that it has happened to others before enables us more easily to accept it.

2. Imposed Change - This is where people are forced to do things they do not wish to do. Examples of this kind of imposed situation include, being imprisoned for breaking the law, paying taxes, paying fines for misdemeanours, clocking in at work and having work rates measured and so on. There is no freedom to choose we must conform or will be punished! Note. For most of us this is not a solution for two reasons. Firstly we only respond to imposed change while we are under control and secondly people who are forced to conform either 'leave their brains at home' or use them to

avoid being controlled.

3. Negotiated Change - This is the province of the facilitator. It is the process through which one individual empowers another to take action to follow a desire or resolve an issue in their lives that they are not 'empowered' to take. This can be permission to do something that the individual is not currently empowered to do, like making a formal presentation or it can be permission to stop doing something damaging to the users health or relationships like stopping smoking or changing value relating style from parent/child to adult.

Negotiated change is a four-step process:-

Step 1 - RECOGNITION - that some belief or behaviour is inappropriate for what we want to achieve now

Step 2 - DECISION - to commit to action to do something about it

Step 3 - PERMISSION - some means of reducing the risk of the change

Step 4 - ACTION - taking action to change the belief or behaviour

The facilitator's role in Action Learning is to empower us to change; to help us 'recognise' a belief or behaviour that has become inappropriate to our current situation and encourage us to decide to change it. To give permission, encourage action and provide, both personally and through our 'comrades in adversity' the support necessary to change it. The key to success in life lies in our ability to adapt to change. Facilitation empowers change. It enables us to become what we want be; to be what we want to become.

Empowering Change

Our current behaviour, the way we handle the different situations we meet in our daily lives, is determined by our values seen through the eyes of our environment, see the 'reinforcement loop. We use the learned behaviours from our past to respond to what is happening now and the results that we achieve from our actions are used to reinforce our role models. This is a closed loop; if I get something right I have done well, if it goes wrong, it's usually someone else's fault. Thus, under normal circumstances, our attitudes and behaviour are self-sustaining; to change we have to break the loop which means questioning the appropriateness of some current action or belief.

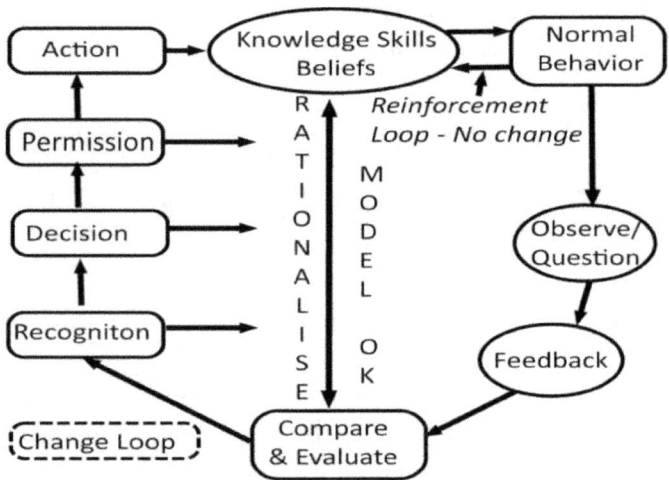

Change starts with questioning. If something that I am doing is not working and I use the question 'why' the door to change is opening. I can do this by questioning myself "Why didn't I get the promotion I was expecting?" Feedback; "They said I did not have enough experience". Compare and Evaluate; Question "Do I have enough experience?" Answer "I don't know". If this leads to 'recognition'

that I need to know what experience I am lacking so that I can do something about it, then I am on the first step of the change ladder.

Step 1 - Recognition

To be successful in life we must be prepared to commit ourselves to a path of ongoing learning. This means assessing both our successes and failures to understand those things we do well and need to do more of and those things which done differently, would produce more desirable outcomes. Such feedback can be 'internal' something that we recognise about ourselves, or it can be 'external', based on the observations of others. For example I may recognise the need to reduce my weight when I stand on the bathroom scales or maybe a friend says 'Put on a bit of weight recently George?' Either input can influence me to think about shedding a few pounds before venturing onto the beach. Feedback which is strong enough to make us question our current behaviour creates the possibility of change. If we accept that some aspect of our current behaviours or beliefs, are inappropriate we have two options; we can accept the feedback in which case we move on to the first step of the change ladder **recognition** or we can reject the input by **rationalising** it.

Some years ago I was flying with what was then recognised as one of the world's leading Airlines in terms of passenger care. The meal was served with style and the wines were good, unfortunately meat was tough and almost cold, but not bad enough to complain about. Later the head steward came through the cabin asking passengers if they had enjoyed their meal, when it was my turn I explained that I had been a little disappointed. His immediate reaction was that he was sorry that I didn't like my meal but that all the other passengers he had spoken to were satisfied! If you don't want feedback you should not ask for it!

Note. Clearly not all feedback is objective or relevant and the ability to rationalise it is, I believe, a key factor in maintaining our self-worth; however overdone rationalisation becomes a barrier to learning. Note - I would like to stress again at this point that in my view human behaviour should not be thought of in terms of right and wrong but as appropriate or inappropriate to the situation. The way we react may well have been appropriate in earlier times but may be currently inappropriate because the circumstances have changed.

Step 2 - Decision

The second step is making the '**decision**' to do something about the behaviour(s) we have identified as no longer appropriate. Making such decisions is easy the problem is implementation. It is easy for me to decide to start my new diet on Sunday; but unfortunately when Sunday comes I realise that it's a 'Ham and Eggs' day and I love my Ham and Eggs, so maybe next Sunday!

I made the decision to go on a diet but am not prepared to make the necessary sacrifice to do it. There can be no gain without pain as the saying goes, if you really want a new you, there are going to be sacrifices. To be successful we must not only decide but be prepared to commit to what we decide. So it's important to be realistic; it's much better to start small and grow big than to start big and fail. Note. We can strengthen our resolve by sharing our decision with others; this increases the pressure on us to act as we don't want to be seen as a 'failure'!

Step 3 - Permission

If I am committed to the '**decision**' to reduce my weight, stop smoking, improve my golf, get a new job, open my own business and so on, I need '**permission**', someone to 'legitimise' my change. Permission is the third step in the process of change and is necessary for two reasons:

1. Our current behaviours and beliefs have been reinforced by apparently successful application throughout our lives. If we are now saying that some of our behaviours are 'inappropriate' to our current situation, we need some 'authority' to change them.
2. Secondly we reduce the risk of failure if we follow the experience of others who have successfully done what we want

to do; their success permits us to do it and can be used to guide us through the process.

We obtain permission by finding 'role models', people who have successfully done what we want to do before. This can come from reading a book, talking to someone who has done it, seeking help from an 'expert'; a professional to improve our golf, a life style coach to get us back in 'shape' or joining one of the plethora of specialist focus sets catering for most every day changes, like stopping smoking, drinking, dieting, fitness and so on. Some years ago I decided to walk the Pennine Way. This is a path which runs for 412km through the Pennine hills in the north of England from just north of Manchester to southern Scotland. The first thing I did was to speak with someone I knew who had walked half of it; the second was to buy a guide book written by a 'recognised expert' on the subject the third was to start walking the five kilometres to work every day to get used to wearing my new boots! Role models give us permission to change; they offer a methodology, a structured approach for achieving our change and they provide support to keep us going when things get tough.

Step 4 - Action

The fourth step in the change process is **action** but it's more than just action, it's about delivery; taking the actions necessary to deliver the desired outcomes. So action is about planning, implementing, monitoring and controlling.

The action or actions you take will clearly depend on what you have decided to change. This can be something as simple as losing weight; simple does not mean easy! This is something you can 'buy' into as it's already 'packaged' and there will normally be a number of competing suppliers. So the first step will be to create some criteria which will allow you to objectively asses the different options. This will include things like price, supplier reputation, convenience – travel, hours etc. The next step is to look at what is on offer, compare the offerings against your criteria and choose a supplier. Implementation in this example means signing on. Once on board you will have weight loss targets which you can use to monitor progress and the set leader will be on hand to encourage and 'control' your achievement until you reach your goal weight.

Note. For most of us changing behaviour takes time; how much time depends on the type of change and our motivation to achieve it. If we are dedicated we can do it alone.

Twenty years ago my wife, a lifelong smoker, had a serious bout of Bronchitis during which she decided for the sake of her health to stop smoking; she has never smoked since.

However most of us need some help. Old habits die hard as the saying goes and we need time to become comfortable with new way of doing things and support on the journey that facilitation and our 'comrades in adversity provide.

Note 'Packaged' change programmes fall into two categories, those which provide ongoing support until the behavioural change has been achieved like 'stop smoking', dieting programmes, AA, life style programmes etc. and those which provide an 'introduction' to the change you would like to make. For example if you need to develop your Presentation Skills as part of getting to the new you, you can start the process by attending a Presentation Skills Workshop. This will provide you with the opportunity to identify what you need to do to become a competent presenter. To achieve this competency however you will need regular practice with feedback over a period time; this needs to be factored into your plan.

So for example before attending a workshop on presentation skills you might negotiate with you manager to let you give his / her monthly staff presentations. If you are seeking to develop your interviewing skills you might ask the HR manager if you can conduct some job interviews after the training and so on. This period of practice is necessary to embed to the new behaviours you wish to adopt.

Note. Some years ago I was asked to help a young man who was going to make a presentation at school to develop his presentation skills. We started the training at nine on a Saturday morning with a discussion on the process and skills of presentation. He then made his first presentation which he had prepared and I gave him feedback using video and a presentation assessment sheet. We continued this with a new presentation every hour until early evening by which time he had mastered the art of presenting.

Creating an Appropriate Learning Environment

The first task of the facilitator is to create a development vehicle through which participants' will experience the things they need to know or to be able to do to be successful in a specific role; we then use this experience to identify and satisfy learning needs. For example, if we want to develop someone's sales skills we need to expose the learner to sales situations, researchers, to research, managers to management. Ah, you may say, we do that now! And to some degree we do, what we don't do is to capture the learning needs and turn them into a development opportunity. To achieve this we need to make learning as important as the doing. We do 'sow' the seeds of a learning process when we expose people to new experiences but we don't, in most cases; reap the harvest by facilitating the learning.

Creating a learning environment starts with an understanding of the learning process. Learning is a two sided coin; on the one side we have 'learning about' and on the other we have 'learning how to'. Leaning 'about' is the simplest of the two because it's concerned with adding knowledge and does not require behavioural change. We learn about our history, we learn another language, we learn about Costing and Budgeting and so on. Note - simple does not mean easy!

Learning 'how to' however is different in that it requires us to do things differently or to do different things and in some cases requires us to believe different things. If we take the example of someone learning to drive, learning the Highway Code only requires us to learn about the 'rules and signs' of the road' to be able to answer the examiners questions when we take the test. However driving the care requires physical co-ordination. At one stage in my life I worked as a driving instructor and found that many learners had initial difficulty in managing the clutch because it required co-ordinating one's feet in an unfamiliar way; but this is a simple action and can be acquired by most learners with a little practice. However physical skill are only one part of the 'how to' component; to be able to interact successfully with others we may also have to change our behaviours which often means changing our values. This is a far more difficult process because it challenges our existing values, which means it takes time and effort to achieve.

From this we can see that there are four components in the learning process which lead to competence:

> Knowledge – Knowing the things we need to know
> Skills – Having the skills to do what we need to do
> Experience – Acquiring the practice to enlighten the theory
> Behaviour - Being able to use the behaviours necessary for success

Thus to be an effective learning vehicle our learning 'environment' must provide the opportunity for participants to test their Knowledge, Skills, Experience and Behaviour (KSEB) as they work through their 'project' and be encouraged to take the appropriate actions where these things are found to be wanting.

The traditional approach to learning has been through teaching 'about' things. Someone does some research to find out what people need to know to be able to do a specific task, like being a manager and they create a programme to provide the necessary knowledge and use this to 'train' people to be managers.

Some years ago I participated in a three year Management Development programme in which we learnt about things like Management, Finance, Human Behaviour, Sales & Marketing, Economics, et al. I personally found the programme very interesting because my background is technical and whilst I was in a middle management position at the time I knew little about these things; the experience added the theory to my practice. However for many of my colleagues, who were actually accountants, HR professionals, Sales and Marketing specialists etc. the parts of the programme which covered their specialism were tedious and in many cases they knew more about the subject than the teacher because they were doing it in practice. Secondly our assignments were based on case studies rather than the real world of work thus the 'answers' often did not accord well with our realities. Thirdly there was no formal structure through which we could use the enormous amount of talent amongst the participants to 'learn with and from each other'; we had to do this over coffee.

Revan's concept of Action learning is based on his belief that practicing managers learn best (about management) 'with and from other managers' rather than by listening to management theory presented by, in his words 'people who had never managed anything'. The learning 'vehicle' that he created, now referred to as Action Learning was based on the idea that managers could best be helped to identify their management learning needs by working on a project which involved them in a real managerial task. To ensure that such projects are 'real'; a senior manager who has the authority to implement the learner's recommendations, gives the learner a 'real' task. These projects are 'long term' normally six months or more and participants meet regularly with a facilitator, to learn 'with and from each other'. In practice projects are usually structured in three parts. Stage one requires the learner to carry out an investigation on behalf of the client '. So for example the client may be looking to reduce the cost of producing a particular product by 20%, getting into a new market or improving productivity etc. The learner is required to investigate the viability of what the client wishes to do and recommend action(s). The second stage of the project requires participants to present their ideas, based on their investigation, to the client and make recommendations on what the client should do. In the third stage the participant will, on behalf of the client, implement the recommendation that have been approved. The project is written up as a set of Terms of Reference which define what the learner will do and the reporting relationship between learner and client. Such a project exposes the learner to all aspects of the management process thus providing a practical framework against which the learner can assess their knowledge, skills, experience and behaviour.

Note.

1. It is important for the success of the learning process to understand the underlying philosophy of the Action Learning project. The investigation phase is designed to create commitment of the learner the decision phase to gain the commitment of the client and the implementation phase to provide the learner with the opportunity to work through the real problems of putting their ideas into practice. Investigation is a bit like courtship; decision is bit like deciding to marry and implementation is like marriage after the honeymoon! So the journey through an Action Learning programme gets harder as you progress; investigation does not 'hurt' anyone's interests but implementation means change for others. To be successful in implementation the learner not only needs to know what we want to achieve, they must also have the behavioural skills to 'sell' it

2. Whilst traditional Action Learning programmes follow the procedure outlined above the model can also be used where the learner is already committed to a specific course of action. We ran a very successful programme for Roche Pharma taking people who had identified their leadership development needs in a London Business School Assessment Centre workshop and used facilitated learning to help them achieve their personal development goals, see - Action Learning Research and Practice 09/2005; 2(2):197-204. DOI: 10.1080/14767330500207043

The structure of the learning environment depends on the focus of the programme. The key is to create the conditions that will ensure that participants have the opportunity to experience the application of the different knowledge and skills they will need to be competent in the role. The review meetings that take place during the journey provide the opportunity for the participants to identify development needs and take appropriate action where necessary. Thus a participant who is competent in finance does not need further training but the same person may need training in how to negotiate win/win solutions. In this way learners are exposed through the action required of them by their projects to the real world and are able to identify with the help of the facilitator their real development needs.

There are a wide range of possibilities but at its simplest level we can divide programmes into two sets, general and specific. General programmes are those which provide participants with development across a range of knowledge, skills, experience and behaviours and specific programmes where the need is known and focuses the development process. In Action Learning terms a sponsor wishing to develop his / her first line managers would be offered an 'own job' programme through which participants identify those things that they do not know or do well now and focus on improving their performance. However where a specific need has been identified, for example a need to improve productivity the programme would focus specifically on this and thus the development of the participants would centre on knowledge, skills, experience and behaviours necessary to improve productivity.

For more detail on programme design please see our books Applications of Action Learning and In-Plant Action Learning.

Facilitation

A group is just a group, a project team is just a project team and the learning opportunities pass by unnoticed or ignored unless we do something to capture and action them. This is the role of the facilitator. He/she, like the grit in the oyster, creates the learning 'pearl'. The facilitator is an 'enabler' not a 'leader'. He/she is concerned with process, the 'how' of doing, not the 'what' of the task.

In Action Learning the 'set' is the learning vehicle and facilitator is the 'driver'. He / she provides the framework for learning. Each participant is given the opportunity to report progress in their project, to identify those things that are going well reflecting competence and those things that are not going so well indicating a need to acquire competence. The set is encouraged to probe these areas to help colleagues 'recognise' the development opportunities which are turned into actions that will be tested and reported on at the next meeting.

There are four parts to the role of the facilitator in Facilitated Learning programmes:

1. Design the programme and run the Introductory Workshop
2. Co-ordinate set meetings
3. Develop the set into a team and
4. Facilitate the recognition of learning needs and encourage and supporting the learning process.

Note. These are normally integrated into one and carried out by a professional facilitator. In our case, because we have focused primarily on large scale programmes aimed at combining organisational change with personal development, we have therefore worked with self-managed teams. This has led us to separate the roles in order to provide practical guidelines which enable sets to be responsible for co-ordinating their meetings, managing team working and the facilitation of their own learning.

The Introductory Workshop

We will assume that the organisational part of the programme is done. We have clients, participants and projects. The facilitator will normally start by reviewing the learning projects which have been agreed between the client and the participants to ensure that they are achievable and the planning of the introductory workshop. Such workshops can vary in length between half a day during which participants are given an introduction to the philosophy of facilitated learning (Action Learning) and an outline of the programme. This is followed by personal introductions, the sharing of projects and the development of initial actions. However such workshops can be extended to include training on things like Meetings Management, Interviewing Skills, Presentations et al, see examples in A*nnex A*. Note. If the programme envisages a number of self-managing sets time will need to be spent during the introductory workshop to familiarising participants with the Coordination, Set Development and Facilitation roles.

Co-ordinating set meetings

The Introductory Workshop is used to 'launch' the programme. By the end of this workshop participants will be in their sets, they will have got to know each other, shared their projects and agreed the action they will take prior to the first meeting. If we are dealing with a single set the facilitator will normally undertake the roles of Co-ordinator, Set Development and Facilitator. For the sake of clarity and because we often have multiple sets where participants are responsible for facilitating their own meetings we will discuss the roles separately.

As was said earlier the set meeting is the focal point for learning; it is during these meetings that learning needs are identified and actions agreed so the way these meetings are run and the recording of agreed action is important. Thus the co-ordinator is responsible for:-

- Planning
- Co-ordination – Running the Meeting
- Minuting
- Reviewing

Planning

This is a simple process; meeting dates and times are normally agreed in advance. The agenda is based on the action plans of individual members. The co-ordinator needs only to ensure that the minutes of the previous meeting are available, the room is prepared and the coffee booked.

Running the meeting

Set meetings follow a 'standard' procedure. The co-ordinator welcomes everyone; then invites one participant at a time to share what they have done since the last meeting. Participants start with a review of what they have done and not done since the last meeting. The review then moves on to a discussion of what has gone well and why? This is followed by the participant being encouraged to reflect on what has not gone so well and why? Note. It is particularly important to look for rationalisation at this stage and probe to find the 'real' reason. The things that do not go well are the pointers to the participant's learning needs and must be fully explored to create understanding from which Areas for Improvement (AFI's) can be agreed.

Each participant usually has 20/30 minutes of personal 'air time'. Set members are encouraged to question and share relevant experiences, with the focus on the actions they took to resolve similar issues and the results achieved. Note. It is a good idea to change the order in which set members report back from meeting to meeting.

Time keeping is important. All members are entitled to their share of the 'air time' so the co-ordinator needs to encourage members to work through their agenda's in the allotted time. If something of general interest comes up it can be moved to the end of the session.

The co-ordinator should listen carefully to what is being said, encourage questioning, particularly the use of open questions and carefully monitor the body language to ensure that all members are actively listening to what is being said. If some members don't appear to be involved the co-ordinator should not hesitate to bring them in. Similarly if a member looks unhappy with the way the discussion is going but is not saying very much the co-ordinator might say - "Fred, you don't look very happy..." Making sure that everyone in involved and that all views are brought out into the open ensures good quality debate which helps the learner to identify his/her development needs.

Co-ordinators should keep in mind the need to be polite and sensitive to the feelings of others. It never hurts to say please and thank you. Being positive about someone's contribution takes little effort but can make a big difference to the attitude people's attitudes to the meeting. Finally agree the date time and place of the next meeting and the next co-ordinator.

Minuting

At the end of the meeting the co-ordinator presents a summary of the proceedings and confirms the arrangements for the next meeting. The minutes should provide a record of what members have committed themselves to do prior to the next meeting and serves as the agenda for the next meeting. Copies should be sent to all members as soon as practical after each meeting. The following is an example of minutes taken during an 'Own Job' set meeting:

Set 1 – First Meeting

Martyn -	Introduce Performance Management with regular interviews
John -	Develop plans for communicating my new role.
Wendy P -	Improve communication in the team with the aim of improving individual commitment.
Heidi -	Negotiate changes to create a more productive environment. Hold regular performance reviews.
James -	Develop myself in my new role (Resource manager)
Wendy -	I will introduce monthly performance reporting in my team.
Alison -	Agree team values. Run problem solving meetings. Introduce more effective ways of working. Manage my interim appraisal to ensure that it benefits me. (Continue to develop my presentation skills)
Shane -	Team development – Apply a performance management approach.

Reviewing

The co-ordinator uses the following form to obtain feedback on how well they have handled the meeting. Members should complete the form individually and discuss to agree their views.

Note. The aim of the meeting review is to provide the opportunity to identify learning points that can then be used to improve the way the meetings are run. This process can be applied to any formal meeting in any environment.

Meeting Feedback Form

1. Was everyone encouraged to be open and participate fully in the process?   Poor 1 2 3 4 5 6 7 8 9 10 Good
2. Did we listen actively to each other and show we understood?   Poor 1 2 3 4 5 6 7 8 9 10 Good
3. Were probing questions designed to aid the learning process encouraged?

Poor 1 2 3 4 5 6 7 8 9 10 Good
4. Did we get value from our time together with everyone having an equal share? Poor 1 2 3 4 5 6 7 8 9 10 Good
5. Was the facilitator supportive in helping us understand our issues and learn from them? Poor 1 2 3 4 5 6 7 8 9 10 Good
6. Were we encouraged to learn from each other's experiences? Poor 1 2 3 4 5 6 7 8 9 10 Good
7. Are you clear what everyone has contracted to do for the next meeting? Poor 1 2 3 4 5 6 7 8 9 10 Good

Note. In self-managed sets the person who co-ordinates the next meeting is normally chosen at this stage and becomes responsible for the circulation of the minutes and the running of the next meeting.

Developing the team

The idea of a learning community where participants learn 'with and from each other' is a very powerful part of Reg's concept of Action Learning. His idea and our experience shows that when the set functions as a team, the members become an integral part of each other's learning process as the following example shows:

Some year ago we were running a programme in Japan with our Japanese partners Chu-San-Ren in which one member had a project to evaluate a new product that his company was planning to invest in. The participant's research suggested that the project was not viable and he was scheduled, the day after the set meeting to go from Nagoya to Tokyo, over 300 miles to make his presentation. He was really terrified because he thought the Chairman would be very unhappy with his findings; so three members of the set volunteered to go to Tokyo with him for support. He made his presentation and Chairman was delighted, he said he also thought it was not a very good idea!

This example highlights the value of support; someone being there for you is a great comfort in stressful times. It also highlights the fact that 'our greatest fears are in our expectations, but these are seldom realised'.

Building the set into a team means encouraging them to work through the following four steps to arrive at 'performing' as soon as possible:

(a) Forming: Why are we here? Set members want to know the purpose and goals of the set. Some may want a formal structure or an agenda while others want to 'play it by ear'. They are trying to get to know each other and begin to understand the size of the problem. Members are polite with one another; leadership moves around, there is little conflict

(b) Storming: This is characterised by set members 'selling' their ideas in a bid to convince the other members to follow their proposed actions. Competition becomes the predominate mode and charges that other members are blocking or not listening are common. Cliques form and reform and are usually at their most powerful during this phase. Hidden agendas are often spotted and commented upon by other set members. There is no great team spirit and the need for the leader to assume the roles of social leader, gatekeeper, and compromiser become important. Unfortunately and the facilitator must be very aware of this, many sets never progress beyond this stage and exist in a bitter state of low level compromises and sub optimal solutions throughout their life.

(c) Norming: The change from stage (b) to (c) is characterised by a change in member's attitudes and behaviours. Attempts to control are met with positive response, sometimes grudgingly. Blocking is substituted by active listening to the other members; and a willingness to change their original positions when presented with honest information about the problem and personal feelings about the set by other members. Team spirit is generated as the barriers go down and this is reinforced as the prospect of developing a helpful solution allows members to begin to want to be a participant in a 'good' team. Creative solutions, using synergy, are developed and constructive questioning, summarising and clarifying is encouraged.

(d) Performing: The set shows high morale and intense loyalty. There is a high degree of empathy between members. There is little need for overt approval as each member appreciates the others and accepts them as individuals. Consequently, creativity is high. The set is effectively "closed" so any new member joining may damage the esprit and cause it to regress to an earlier phase.

Creating the level of trust and openness necessary for the set to function effectively can sometimes be difficult. Individuals from different backgrounds and differing loyalties are being asked to be open and trust each other in a situation of shared authority. Moving from 'forming' to 'storming' means risking the consequences of inter personal conflict, personal attacks. Moving from 'storming' to 'norming' means beginning to accept each other's point of view and starting to look for workable comprise. To move from 'norming' to 'performing' members have to trust each other, and risk having that trust broken. This can be a risky business and there is usually some pain. But there is always a risk associated with real learning and development sets need to go through these stages if they are to reach the level openness where they can rise above the interpersonal and focus their energies on the task.

Figure 1

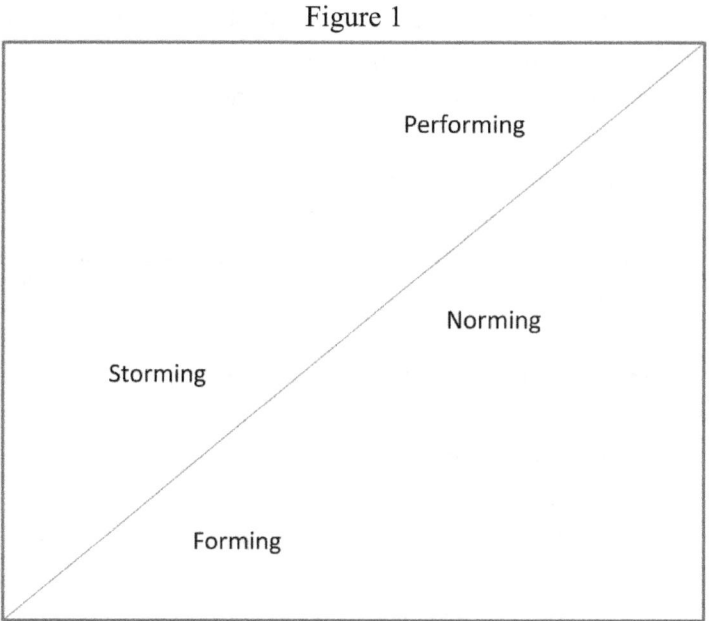

Psychologist Bruce Tuckman first came up with this memorable phrase "forming, storming, norming, and performing" in his 1965 article, "**Developmental Sequence in Small Groups**."

It is important that facilitators are aware of these stages in set development and are able to recognise them. The facilitator's task is to help the set reach the 'performing' stage as quickly as possible. This may sound easy, but in practice it is not so simple. The model in fig. 1 suggests that sets move logically through the stages but in fact they do not. They tend to jump from one to the other and back again depending how they feel. The set may be 'performing' today but tomorrow may go right back to 'storming' for no apparent reason. This is because the way relationships develop is subconscious; members don't consciously know the level they have reached and therefore don't know it has regressed. It is the facilitator's task to make members conscious of this process. Each stage needs to be highlighted and seen as a stepping-stone. Once the set has stepped over it and recorded that step there is no need to revisit it.

The facilitator's role is to help the set see itself, how it is working and how this can be improved by bringing the unconscious into the conscious through questioning and challenging what is going on.

The following are some of the reasons why this can be difficult

- Members are more concerned with providing answers than exploring problems
- Lack of questioning and listening
- Meeting dominated by strong personalities
- No attempt to follow a logical process
- Desire not to be involved
- Lack of testing of understanding or summarising
- Lack of direction by the co-ordinator

Once the facilitator has identified the key issues in the way the set is functioning he/she must decide the most effective method of collecting evidence. It is important that the facilitator remember the old salesman's adage 'telling isn't selling'. The facilitator is only the agent of change and the goal is to help the set 'recognise' its own problem(s). To achieve this he/she must collect evidence to demonstrate their points. In most situations taking simple notes of what is being said using the presenter's own words will suffice. If the issues is more to do with the way the set is functioning more specific tools may be more appropriate, see **Annex B** for **Tools for Facilitators.**

Facilitating Recognition and Encouraging Learning

Facilitation is key to the success of Action Learning programmes because it focuses on the 'learning' process. Those things participants do well reflect their current competence, those things that do not do so well indicate a need to acquire competence. Thus by sharing the actions they have taken on their project and the results of those actions participants are able, with the help of the facilitator and their 'comrades in adversity' to identify and satisfy their learning needs.

The facilitator is a –

> ✓ Challenger of beliefs
> ✓ Difficulty focuser
> ✓ Catalyst
> ✓ Opportunity promoter
> ✓ Developer of skills - Listening, Questioning, Giving and Receiving critical feedback etc.,
> ✓ Resource suggester
> ✓ In the early stages of the programme, a guide to the future

The Facilitator is not a –

> ✓ Teacher
> ✓ Director
> ✓ Guru
> ✓ Problem Solver
> ✓ Presenter

The facilitator has two main tasks:-

1. To use the situations revealed by participants during the set meetings where things did not go well with the projects to identify learning needs and
2. To encourage participants to take action to resolve them.

In practice this means that whilst the project starts simply as a project, as time goes by it takes on a dual focus with participants working on both their projects and in parallel taking the actions necessary to satisfy their personal development needs.

Facilitation in Practice

The process starts with the first set meeting. This will normally be part of the Introductory Workshop and focuses on 'getting to know' each other. The facilitator introduces themselves and explains that each member will be asked in turn to do the same, Name, Job, background etc. Note. It's useful to provide a proforma for this to ensure commonality. They will them be asked to explain their project and to share what they hope to achieve through their participant in the set. The set are then encouraged by the facilitator to ask questions for clarification finishing with an agreement on the action(s) the participant will take prior to the next meeting; the facilitator records this for the minutes, see example in the section on Minuting and moves on to the next person. When all participants have introduced themselves and agreed their initial actions the meeting closes with an agreement on the time and date of the next meeting.

Facilitation actually begins at the second meeting; now we have some action, some things will have gone well, other not so well. Now we can start to identify learning needs. As was said earlier there are four aspects to competence in any given situation:

Knowledge – We have to know about the thing that we would like to do. It is not possible to make a competent presentation about Mountaineering, Politics, Equal Opportunities et al or drive a car, fly an aeroplane, sail across the Atlantic, unless you know something about it.

Skills – We need the mental and physical skills to be able to, drive a car, sail a boat, fly an aeroplane etc.

Experience - Is the practice of doing which provides the wisdom of 'knowing what we are talking about.

Behaviours – Behaviour is shaped by our values; these create our attitudes which 'trigger' behaviours. To change our behaviour we need to modify our values to change our attitudes thus enabling us to behave in the way which is appropriate to our desired outcomes.

The facilitator is looking for competence in these four areas and seeking to encourage learning where there is a need. This is achieved by using the experiences generated by the project to empower participants to identify their learning needs. The role of the facilitator is to encourage set members to question each other openly on both their successes and failures and where things have not gone well to explore the reasons why using the KSEB model.

Did the participant who failed to get agreement on some change they were proposing to their client fail because they did not have:

1. Sufficient knowledge to make a compelling case?
2. The skills to present a winning argument?
3. The experience to support their arguments?
4. The behavioural competence necessary to manage the relationship?

The reason or reasons for failure could be any of these or indeed more than one; it is the job of the facilitator to encourage participants to probe what happed and why. Once there is common understanding of the issue(s) the facilitator moves the discussion on to action, what the participant will 'do' to resolve the issue. The agreed actions are minuted and are used to assess progress on what is now the individual's 'Personal Development' project.

This meeting follows a similar process to the first meeting except that the:

1. Agenda is based on the minutes of the previous meeting
2. Order of the discussion is changed to give variety to the process
3. Focus now is on using the actions taken on the 'client' project to identify and agree actions to resolve learning needs

Participants are asked to talk about the actions they set themselves at the previous meeting, what went well, what did not go so well and why? All participants are encouraged by the facilitator to participate in the discussion and share relevant experiences. Once the issues are clear the participants whose project is being discussed is asked to identify the actions they plan to take prior to the next meeting. These actions are recorded and the discussion moves the next person. When all participants have spoken about their projects and agreed their next actions, the meeting closes with an agreement on the time and date of the next meeting. Note. The facilitator then prepares and circulates the minutes. This is important because it reinforces 'peer set' pressure; everyone knows what I said I would do, therefore I will look very foolish if I haven't done it! See the following example of a Personal Development Plan.

Typical Personal Development action plan

Personal Development
Terms of Reference Form

Name: – John Williams

Title of Project: - Improve working relationship with peers

Current Situation: - *Describe the opportunity to be taken or the issue to be resolved.*

The understanding/working relationship between me and my peers should be improved.

Purpose: - *What do you want to achieve through the action?*

Improve working relationship with peers by increasing mutual understanding of our motivations/priorities. By doing so, I will train / improve my situational leadership skills.

Activities: - *What actions will you undertake? By when? (Please be specific about dates)*

Meeting for coffee and having lunch more often (minimum once a week) start immediately and on-going (write log of activities)

Apply tools (like Belbin, WIS) to "characterize" them (having finished first round by mid-November); later-on regular check and up-date

Practice open questioning (start immediately)

1. Reflect and write-down open questioning activities (minimum once a week)
2. Get performance feedback from my Learning Set
3. Get feedback from my Coach (Marc)
4. Join Coaching course

a) Use my Learning Set to validate my perception and to get other insights when I am unsure about interpreting a situation

b) As a second step, learn more about other tools to be used. Start January as soon as Belbin and WIS "characterization" has been "validated"

What resources do you consider necessary? People, money, time, etc.

a) One additional hour per week to reflect and write down log of activities

b) Time over coffee and lunch (not additional)

c) Get permission (money) to join coaching course

d) Take 2 additional hours every month for Learning Set discussions

What form will the outcome take? (A report, presentation etc.?)

a) Improved/more specific 360 feedback from same peers

b) Better feeling about the mutual understanding

At this point in the process participants have two projects, their Client project and their Personal Development project. From this point on both will be discussed in the set meetings and the minutes will reflect the actions agreed. In the following example Sally started the programme with feedback from her manager that he would like her to improve the way she was working with her team. At the second meeting she admitted that she had not really done much because she was unsure how to go about it. During that discussion it emerged that John had been in a similar situation when he was promoted to team leader a couple of years earlier and he had resolved the problem by introducing a series of meetings including a monthly 'one on one' meeting with all of his people. He had also attended a short Communication Skills development programme run by the in house-trainer. It was agreed that John would talk with Sally about what he did and she would create a process model for her department.

> Sally – Do what I should have done last time - Improve regular communication with my team. I will start by going to see what John is doing and talk with some of his team to find out how they feel about it. I will then write a proposal for my team and talk with my manager about it.

As the meetings progress so the need for external involvement decreases. Participants become increasingly aware of the value of reflection and develop the skills necessary to manage the learning process for themselves; indeed where we have run ongoing programmes we have had no difficulty finding people who have been through the experience who are happy to facilitate new sets.

Can you be a Facilitator?

The answer for most of us is yes, you can. So what do you need to know and be able to do?

Knowledge

The facilitator needs to know about:

The learning process and how it works

Facilitation is concerned with helping people to change. Some of our Knowledge, Skills, Experience and Behaviours are appropriate to our current situation but others are inappropriate for the things we now want to achieve. For example, most of us are brought up to 'follow' so moving from 'doing' to managing others means that some of our current behaviours are no longer appropriate and we need to replace them with others that are appropriate to our new situation.

If we take the case of the young man we discussed in the previous chapter. He had been very successful in getting to a senior specialist position in the company because of his 'technical' ability. Suddenly he found himself in a situation where he needs the cooperation of others to be successful. To be effective in his new role he must now focus on creating relationships, something he did not need to do before. Now he is faced with the need 'sell' himself to his peers. He **recognises** *this need so he is on the first rung of the change ladder. The second step is* **decision***; the fact that he has joined Learning Set means that he has made the decision to change. His TOR indicates that he feels empowered; he has* **permission** *to do things and he has a list of* **actions** *so he is in the process of change.*

Over the next few months with the support and encouragement of the facilitator and his 'comrades in adversity' set he was able to create a good working relationship with both his peers and his own team.

For a more detailed understanding of the nature and process of change we recommend our new book Change; Become a Winner which available from Amazon

The design and management of programmes

I include this 'knowledge base' for the sake of completeness. I covered it earlier in the book in the chapter on 'Creating the Learning Environment' so there is no need to repeat it here. I will only add that if you are seeking to create an Own job or In-Plant Action learning programme you will find everything you need to know in our two books, see our website www.ala-international.com

The process they are facilitating

Having an understanding of what the participant is going through and the problems they are facing is I believe necessary for developing rapport. The fact that you have 'been there' legitimises you in the role. I have been facilitating Action Learning sets where the primary focus has been the development of managerial knowledge and skills for over thirty years; I spent the twenty years before that developing my managerial skills. Having been there, done it and got the 'T' shirt provides the credibility necessary to give 'permission' to change.

Where to find the resources participants will need along the way

It is not part of the 'classical' role of the facilitator to provide advice on how participants should satisfy their development needs. However I personally feel that the facilitator needs some knowledge about the 'process of things' in order to be able to ask enlightening questions.

Some year ago I was working on what we call an In-Plant programme where we had a number of sets working on specific projects aimed at improving productivity. One of the projects was focused on reducing the change over time for a large printing press. At the start of the project the changeover was taking twenty-four hours, the goal for the team was to halve that. During the first meeting it became clear that when I asked if the target was achievable no one really knew what was possible. This simple question led them to decide that their first task must be to find out. They did this by asking the manufacturer of the press for information about other companies who had bought the same machine. They found twelve similar machines in Europe and made contact with the people involved. From their research they identified one machine in Sweden and one in Germany where the users reported eight hour, or one shift changeovers. They asked for and received permission to go and watch a changeover in both companies. As a result of this experience they were able to make recommendations to their own management which led them achieving some months later a changeover time of six hours.

Skills

The facilitator needs to be able to;

Deliver a workshop

In my experience the facilitator is also a trainer. At the start of the programme the only person who knows what is going on is the facilitator, so he or she must be able to run the Introductory Workshop. The ability to do this can also be valuable where the facilitator has specific skills, in my case it would be in management and interpersonal skills, for the facilitator to be able to offer a training module where common needs are identified in the set.

Manage meetings

This goes without saying as it is an integral part of the role at least in the early stages.

Develop Relationships

The facilitator must be able to create and maintain interpersonal relationships both on an individual and team level. This means being able to:

1. develop rapport
2. ask both open and closed questions to elicit information
3. listen intelligently, observe the meta messages and understand the meaning
4. Understand the 'Tools of Team working' set out in the next chapter and be able to select appropriate tools for specific situations
5. empathise and encourage introspection
6. create a climate of empowerment through participation
7. use assertiveness techniques to deliver win / win outcomes

Experience

I believe that to be effective the facilitator needs to have at least some experience of:

The participant's situation

I feel that this is necessary in order to be able to empathise with the learner as he / she works through their project. I feel that having shared experience with the learner(s) and the credibility this brings is a key factor in the relationship. Clearly one will not have shared experiences for all situations but in my experience there almost certainly someone in the set who either does or knows someone who does.

Experience of Life

A key part of the facilitation process is 'permission'. The changes that the facilitator has experienced in their lives and what they have learnt from them, provides the 'permission' for others to change.

Managing change

As was said earlier, some changes are easier than others primarily because they have less impact on our values. Thus learning how to create a budget is a matter of simple routine, however learning to make winning presentation is different because for most people it requires an attitude change. The actual process is simple but changing our values from 'You're OK I'm not OK' to 'You're OK I'm OK' takes time and effort. So it is important, when a development need is identified in the set that the facilitator encourages participants to seek solution that are appropriate to the level of change required.

Behaviour

Our values determine our attitudes which govern our behaviour. The things we value and those things we do not value, determines what we are. To be an effective facilitator it seems to me that one must be:

1) Committed to the process of helping others to learn
2) Aware of oneself and others
3) Insightful, able to see the real picture
4) Open to the values and beliefs of others
5) Tolerant of ambiguity,
6) Constructive, prepared to share and debate to achieve understanding
7) Able to 'let go' when the job is done

Getting Started

Facilitating Learning is a very rewarding experience. Working with people who want to learn is extremely satisfying. Helping people to recognise that it is not 'someone else's fault' when things go wrong, it's 'mine' and I can do something about it. I can be more effective and by being more effective I can have a more fulfilling life.

Are you a natural facilitator? Why not start with a self-assessment? Choose a process you would like to facilitate. It can be a life style change, you know someone who is looking to change; they would like to stop doing something or start something new and you would like to help. It can be about helping someone improve their performance, like playing better golf, or simply personal development.

I would like to …

Now profile yourself imaging that you are in the role of facilitating someone who is in the situation you have described and ask yourself the question 'Will xxx see me as credible in this role?'

Knowledge

Do I know:

About the learning process and how it works - Yes / Partially / No
How to design and manage programmes- Yes / Partially / No
The process I would like to facilitate - Yes / Partially / No
Where to find the resources participants will need - Yes / Partially / No

Skills

Am I able to:

Deliver a workshop - Yes / Partially / No
Manage meetings - Yes / Partially / No

Develop Relationships -

1. develop rapport - Yes / Partially / No
2. ask both open and closed questions to elicit information - Yes / Partially / No
3. listen intelligently, observe the meta messages and understand the meaning - Yes / Partially / No
4. Understand the 'Tools of Team working' set out in Annex B and am able to select appropriate tools for specific situations - Yes / Partially / No
5. empathise and encourage introspection - Yes / Partially / No
6. create a climate of empowerment through participation - Yes / Partially / No
7. use assertiveness techniques to deliver win/win outcomes - Yes / Partially / No

Experience

Do I have some experience of:

The situation that the people or person I would like to help is in - Yes / Partially / No
Does my experience qualify me to facilitate others - - Yes / Partially / No
Do I really understand the Nature and Process of Change - Yes / Partially / No

Behaviour

Am I:

1. Committed to the process of helping others to learn - - Yes / Partially / No

2. Aware of oneself and others - Yes / Partially / No
3. Insightful, able to see the real picture - Yes / Partially / No
4. Open to the values and beliefs of others - Yes / Partially / No
5. Tolerant of ambiguity, - Yes / Partially / No
6. Constructive, prepared to share and debate to achieve understanding - Yes / Partially / No
7. Able to 'let go' when the job is done - Yes / Partially / No

Now review your profile, what does it tell you? If you are competent at developing relationships and the facilitating behaviours you have the skills and value set to facilitate learning. Knowledge and experience are task specific, if you are coaching (facilitating) your local football team they will expect you to have knowledge and experience of football. Equally if you decide to decide to join a dieting set you would expect the facilitator to be a role model.

If you have the knowledge and experience and would like to develop your facilitation skills you can join a Learning Set, there are plenty about and today many are online. In the Action Learning world you can contact IFAL, The International Foundation for Action Learning at admin@ifal.co.uk. IFAL has affiliate organisations in many different countries that will be happy to help. You can try LinkedIn at www.linkedin.com or contact the World Institute for Action Learning at www.wial.org/action-learning or you can Google facilitation skills training for more options.

If you believe that you have the skills to get started, try it for yourself. It doesn't have to be formal; you can start with friends and family. The next time someone says to you 'I had a terrible day yesterday...' Instead of saying poor you, you can say. Tell me a bit about it... Try it, it's easy and remember 'the answer is always in the question' the right question will tell you everything you need to know.

Use your facilitating skills to help others to help themselves. Bon courage et bon chance.

Annex A – Example Introductory Workshop Programmes

Example 1

Introduction to Action Learning

INTRODUCTION

Action learning is a process which empowers personal development. It provides a supportive environment in which individuals who are seeking to develop themselves can share experiences and help each other to achieve their personal goals. XXX has decided to introduce Action Learning as a tool for enhancing the effectiveness of the L2+ Modular Leadership Skills Development programme. The aim is to provide participants with learning support when they return to work underpinning the individual learning opportunities presented by the L2+ modules and their transfer into improved performance in the workplace. Programmes will be organised and facilitated by the local HR community on each site and participants who have experienced the process and would, as a result, like to help others learn.

This workshop is designed to provide an overview of the process and show how it can help you to achieve the goals of your personal action plan.

OBJECTIVES

1. To explain the concept of the Action Learning programme
2. To show how it works in practice
3. To create a number of pilot sets on each site

FOR

Sponsoring managers and past participants of the L2+ programme

METHOD

The Action Learning approach will be used throughout. This is based on three guiding principles:

- ❑ Human beings learn best from reflected practice.
- ❑ The best test of any learning is trying it out in action.
- ❑ The process of learning is greatly strengthened by regularly sharing the experience with others who are also learning by doing.

PROGRAMME CONTENT

- ❑ Introduction to the Action Learning programme
- ❑ The nature and process of change
- ❑ Creating an effective set
- ❑ The role of the co-ordinator / facilitator
- ❑ Clarifying your purpose
- ❑ Effective communication – Active listening / using questions / The 3 step approach to assertiveness
- ❑ Beliefs
- ❑ Open forum discussion

PROGRAMME

Introductory Workshop – ½ day

1100 – 1115   Introduction and Programme Objectives
1115 – 1230   What is Action Learning?
1230 – 1330   Lunch
1330 – 1500   Getting Started – GB/RL and Facilitators
1500 – 1530   Agreeing the Way Ahead – Participants and
Facilitators
1530   Review and Close

EVALUATION

On completion of the workshop participants will have:-
- ✓ An understanding of the Action Learning process and how it will work
- ✓ Identified whether they would like to be part of the process
- ✓ Agreed the structure, timings and membership of local sets

----

Example 2

INTRODUCTORY WORKSHOP PROGRAMME

INTRODUCTION

This programme is designed as a launch workshop for In-Plant project sets. The workshop sets out the role of the team in the problem solving process and provides a structured approach that can be used to guide them through the project

OBJECTIVES

- ✓ To ensure a common understanding of the both the project(s) and the learning goals of the programme.
- ✓ To provide some training in the basic skills
- ✓ To start the project

FOR

The project teams and their facilitators

METHOD

The Action Learning approach will be used throughout. This is based on three guiding principles:

(1)   Human beings learn best from reflected practice.
(2)   The best test of any learning is trying it out in action.
(3)   The process of learning is greatly strengthened by regularly sharing the   experience with others who are also learning by doing.

PROGRAMME CONTENT

- ✓ Open forum discussion about the programme and how it will work
- ✓ The role of the coordinator and facilitator
- ✓ The Investigation stage
- ✓ Describe the situation & set objectives
- ✓ Develop a work plan
- ✓ Collect data - get the facts
- ✓ Analyse the information
- ✓ Define the Problem & Review Objectives
- ✓ Develop alternative solutions
- ✓ Choose one option
- ✓ Conduct a risk analysis
- ✓ Write & present a report outlining the recommendations
- ✓ Starting the project – Reviewing the TOP and meeting the client
- ✓ Open forum discussion

PROGRAMME

Introductory Workshop – 1 day

0900 – 0915 Introduction and Objectives

0915 – 0930 Introduction to Set Problem Solving Process and facilitation

0930 – 1045 Set Problem Solving – Exercise

1100 – 1300 Exercises continued

1400 – 1430 Teams choose coordinator and facilitator.

1430 – 1530 Review TOR and create programme of work

1600 – 1630 Meeting with client(s)

1630 – 1700 Agree tasks and plan next meeting

1700 – 1730 Open forum review and close

EVALUATION

On completion of the workshop participants will have:-
- ✓ A clear understanding of the process and what is expected
- ✓ Appointed a coordinator and a facilitator
- ✓ Produced a programme of work for the Investigation Phase

Annex B - Tools for Facilitators

The following 'tools' can be used to gather evidence on different aspects of Set and Individual performance. Some tools are more appropriate for giving feedback to the set (S), others for giving individual (I) feedback and some are useful for both (B).

Questioning & Listening (B)

This is the simplest and most useful tool in the facilitator's armoury. There are two types of question available; closed question those which begin with, did you, can you, should you, will you, do you? etc. Such questions are closed in that they elicit specific answers, yes or no. Their primary purpose is to confirm situations or events and to provide openings for open question.

Open questions create the opportunity for dialogue which provides information. There are six simple words that reveal all you need to know to understand the person or the situation. They are enshrined in Rudyard Kipling's simple poem 'I keep six honest Serving men'.

> *I keep six honest serving men*
> *(They taught me all I knew);*
> *Their names are What and Why and When*
> *And How and Where and Who...*

Questions 'where do you think you are now with the project' or 'what do you see as the problem' will provide information on how the other person sees the problem; if this is then followed by 'why, you will start to 'drill down' to the real issue.

In the following example, John is late for an important appointment; the client is upset and phones his manager to complain. When John returns to the office his manager asks him 'what' happened. John says 'sorry I got lost'. Manger 'why'? John I couldn't get the GPS to work'. Manager 'why'? The battery was flat...

Having asked the question it's necessary to listen 'actively' to the answer. Active listening means not only listening to the words people use but also to voice tone and observing the non-verbal behaviour, particularly body posture and eye movements. Thus if we ask someone 'How do you feel today?' and they reply fine! We can assume it's true. However if they say not too bad! Maybe things are not OK. If we ask someone 'Are you sure you did xxx?' and they respond positively but look away or speak more quietly when they answer, it's probably not true. We all know, understand and re-act to these non-verbal signals but usually this happens sub-consciously. For the facilitator it is essential to be conscious of these signals and their meaning; they are the key to the door of understanding, the gateway to truth and so to learning.

Note. For examples of questions relevant to working with Action learning Sets please feel free to contact us.

Direct Help (I)

This is where the set is obviously struggling with something and the facilitator leads them through the problem. Maybe they have many ideas but are having difficulty focusing them, or they know what they need to do but find it difficult to agree on how to produce a plan. If the facilitator has the skills they can show them how. But it must be done very skilfully, the facilitator moving into the leader role and out again, transferring it back to the appointed leader when the particular problem is solved. If this is not done well there is a risk that the facilitator will be seen as the leader or will become the victim if the solutions arrived at in the intervention fails.

Rounds (I)

One of the major problems with sets is that it is easy for the powerful to dominate. The 'rounds' technique enables the set process to be more democratic and the weak to be as powerful as the strong. It also reduces the time wasted on unnecessary extended debate. Calling for a 'round' provides the opportunity for any participant to stop the discussion and seek individual opinions. The 'round' empowers each participant, in turn, to state their views on the issue under discussion, without interruption from the others.

If, for example, the set is discussing some action a member has taken or plans to take and there are clearly differing views about it the member, or the facilitator may call for a round to try and clarify what members think about the issue. Each individual then gives his/her perception in turn whilst the others listen. After everyone has contributed the person who called for the round summarises and the meeting continues.

Fight Flight (B)

This is a means of transmitting "unpleasant messages" to individuals or sets which ensures that the receiver(s) owns the message. The basic difficulty when trying to communicate such messages to human beings is that we find ways of rationalising the message so that we don't have to accept it. For example, a manager who is unhappy with the way one of his people has done a particular job may try to tell them that he is unhappy. If we don't like what people say to us we rationalise it, usually by playing 'yes but'. *Yes but you weren't clear what you wanted...., yes but we didn't really have time.... , yes but this is the information we were given.... etc.* The receiver's objective is to rationalise the feedback so that it is not his/their fault.

The 'fight flight' technique enables the facilitator to overcome this problem by acknowledging it. If the facilitator wants to tell the set or an individual member that he/she thinks they are on the wrong track, he/she begins the communication by saying "You probably won't agree with this but I think..." Or "I'm sure you don't see it like this but my perception is ..... Now they have no basis for response because you have already acknowledged that they won't agree. All they can do is consider the message.

Fish Bowl (I)

This technique can be used to make people more aware of their behaviour. At its simplest level a set of people are asked to discuss a specific topic whilst others sit outside the set and observe their behaviour. At the end of a given period of time the observers are asked to play back what they have seen/heard and to comment of what they see as the positive and negative points of the discussion. This is a very useful tool for highlighting set process and individual attitudes.

Set / Set Feedback (S)

This tool is used to provide feedback on how the total set is working. We have chosen one instrument, figure 1, as representative of the many hundreds of instruments which exist in this category because it is both easy for the facilitator to use and for the set to relate to. Basically all the user needs to do is to put a cross under each heading against the particular description which most nearly describes the behaviour of the set. For example under Set Goals, if there appear to be none the cross would be at the left hand end, if they are average in the middle and very clear, on the right.

The instrument can be used in two ways:

a) By the facilitators to feedback on what he/she thinks about the way the set is working.

b) By the set itself to measure its own performance. In this case the set stops its work on the task for a little while and each member is asked to complete the instrument showing his perception of set effectiveness this is then shared as a means of highlighting strengths and weaknesses.

General Feedback Questionnaire

The following questionnaire is designed to provide an objective method for giving performance feedback to sets. It may be used by an external observer or by set members themselves as the basis of an open discussion.

How clear are the group goals?

1.	2.	3.	4.	5.
No apparent goals	Goal confusion, uncertainty or conflict	Average goal clarity	Goals mostly clear	Goals very clear

How much trust and openness was there in the group?

1.	2.	3.	4.	5.
Distrust, a closed group	Little trust, individuals defensive	Average trust and openness	Considerable trust and openness	Remarkable trust and openness

How much attention was given to process? (The way the group organised its work?)

1.	2.	3.	4.	5.
No attention to process	Little attention to process	Some concern with process	A fair balance between task and process	Very concerned with process

What kind of leadership was there in the group?

1.	2.	3.	4.	5.
No leadership	Leadership concentrated in one person	Some leadership sharing	Leadership functions distributed	Leadership needs creatively and flexibly met

How were group decisions made?

1.	2.	3.	4.	5.
No decisions reached	Made by a few	Majority vote	Attempts to integrate different opinions	Full participation and tested consensus

How well were group resources used?

1.	2.	3.	4.	5.
Only one or two people involved	Several tried to contribute but were discouraged	Average use of resources	Group resources used and encouraged	Group resources fully and effectively used

Behaviour Modelling (B)

This focuses on individual behaviour and can be used to provide feedback either on the way the set is being managed or on the behaviour of a particular individual or individuals. It provides the observer with a framework for demonstrating the behaviours being used. The data can then be examined and questions about its effectiveness discussed.

The idea of categorising the verbal statements people make, and giving feedback to improve interpersonal performance was first explored by Bailes (1) in America, over fifty years ago. More recently, the work has been popularised in Britain by Neil Rackham and Peter Honey (2) in their work with British Airways on improving the interpersonal skills and performance of customer liaison staff. The work is based on the concept that it is possible, in any behavioural situation, to identify through analysis the types of behaviour which make people effective. If we then put trainees into the particular situation, for example chairing a meeting, and measure the way they behave, we can provide feedback from an 'expert model' which over time the trainee can learn to use in order to develop and improve performance.

The first step in developing the expertise to use this material is to read and understand the behavioural categories outlined in the Developing Interpersonal Skills (DIS) Observation Sheet. These are general categories and are appropriate for analysing behaviours in meetings, chairmanship and team working situations.

- Content proposals – statements concerned with doing the task
- Procedural proposals – statements concerned with how to do the task
- Building – builds on something others have contributed
- Supporting – statements which support and encourage others
- Disagreeing – arguing against some else's ideas
- Defend / Attack – strongly disagreeing with others

- Open – statements which leave maker open to loss of status or ridicule
- Testing understanding – test what people mean
- Summarising – as it says
- Seeking information – asking questions
- Giving information – making statements
- Bringing in – invites a contribution from others, can be general or specific
- Shutting out - A behaviour which blocks another person's opportunity to participate in the discussion

Once the categories are understood try the following short test.

BEHAVIOUR CATEGORISATION EXERCISE

Listed below are a number of statements made by negotiators during a meeting. In order to check on your interpretation of the behaviour analysis categories please read each statement and tick the category which you think best fits the statement.

1. I suggest that we begin by exploring our position on the overtime issue.

    Building
    Procedural Proposal
    Giving Information
    Testing Understanding

2. So now it's my fault is it? Well let me tell you this
    ......

    Disagreeing
    Seeking/Information
    Defending/Attacking
    Shutting out

3. Can I just check that I've got this right? Are you saying that you must have our full reply by Monday, or that you only need a reply to point 3?

    Seeking Information
    Summarising
    Bringing in
    Testing Understanding

4. Just to recap on that, you are objecting to three things - the manning levels, the work-study proposals and the overtime reduction.

    Summarizing
    Giving Information
    Open
    Disagreeing

5. I'm sorry Mr Lawson, I got a bit heated just then, I didn't mean to imply that you were dishonest and I apologies if I gave that impression.

    Giving Information
    Open
    Defending/Attacking
    Supporting

6. Yes, that's a good idea and I go along with it completely.

    Building
    Giving Information
    Bringing in
    Supporting

7. I think Fred's idea would be even more useful if we included an additional form of access in the central area.

    Building
    Supporting
    Procedural Proposal
    Giving Information

8. Am I right in thinking that twelve machines would be affected if we accepted this recommendation?

    Testing Understanding
    Seeking Information
    Bringing In
    Open

9. We're getting nowhere – I think John is on the wrong track...

    Disagreeing
    Supporting
    Defending/Attacking
    Giving Information

10.   The report we have been asked to consider suggests
       that average earnings in January were £46.50 above budget. I
       suggest we start by investigating the discrepancy
                Bringing in
                Giving Information
                Summarizing
                Content Proposal

11.   Hang on a minute Fred! Mary, you have been very quiet during
       our discussions, what do you think?
                Testing Understanding
                Seeking Information
                Bringing In / Shutting out
                Open

12.   I have discovered that if we use a jig we can halve the time it
       takes to assemble our new filter…
                Building
                Supporting
                Procedural Proposal
                Giving Information

ANSWERS

        1. Procedure Proposal
        2. Defend/Attack
        3. Testing Understanding
        4. Summarizing
        5. Open
        6. Supporting
        7. Building
        8. Seeking Information
        9. Disagreeing
        10. Content Proposal
        11. Bringing in / Shutting out
        12. Giving Information

Now look at the scoring system shown in figure 3. The names of individual participants are written across the top one in each column. Individual contributions are categorised by the observer and a figure 1 is placed in the appropriate box. So from the example we can see that, in these observations, Les has 5 task proposals, Anne 2, Keith 5, Mark none and so on. Each contribution is categorised and recorded in the appropriate box with one stroke no matter how long it lasts. So if Anne says "Do we want to tell Fred that we no longer wish to work with him?" That's testing understanding and would score one mark in the appropriate box.

The observation should be done as a series of short, ten to fifteen minute, timed snap shots. This provides a view of what has happened at different times, showing how things have developed. Scores are added vertically, to show total individual contribution and horizontally showing contribution by category. The analysis is concerned with highlighting, behaviour by type, level of contribution and leadership or controlling behaviours, those used by the 'leader'. Individuals who are high in the following categories are portraying controlling behaviour.

> Procedural proposals, supporting, open, testing understanding, summarising, asking questions, bringing in and shutting out.

Feedback is normally given by the observer as a series of statements about set behaviour supported by the 'model'. For example, in the first set of observations we can see that Anne is leading the set but in the second set of observations there is no clear leadership.

Once you feel comfortable with the idea take a copy of the blank scoring sheet figure 5, find a small active set and test the approach out. It will take time at first to build competency but this will soon come if you stick at it. Once you feel confident with your data start to share it with the set.

DEVELOPING INTERPERSONAL SKILLS (DIS)
OBSERVATION SHEET (Fig 3)

Date   Group
Observer   Activity

Name												
CONTENT PROPOSALS												
PROCEDURAL PROPOSALS												
BUILDING												
SUPPORTING												
DISAGREEING												
DEFEND/ ATTACK												
OPEN												
TESTING UNDERSTANDING												
SUMMARISING												
SEEKING INFORMATION												
GIVING INFORMATION												
BRINGING IN												
SHUTTING OUT												
TOTAL												

INPLANT™ ACTION LEARNING

DEVELOPING INTERPERSONAL SKILLS (DIS)
OBSERVATION SHEET

Date 12/7/99   Group /

Observer George   Activity BUILD A STRUCTURE

	LES	ANNE	KELLY	MARK						
CONTENT PROPOSALS	IIII	II	IIII							
PROCEDURAL PROPOSALS		III								
BUILDING		II								
SUPPORTING	I	III	II	III						
DISAGREEING	I		I							
DEFEND/ ATTACK										
OPEN		II								
TESTING UNDERSTANDING		III								
SUMMARISING		II								
SEEKING INFORMATION	II	IIII	II	II						
GIVING INFORMATION	III	I	I	II						
BRINGING IN		I								
SHUTTING-OUT										
TOTAL	12	22	11	7						

References

1. Interaction Process Analysis, Bailes R.F. Addison Wesley Press - 1951
2. Developing Interactive Skills ed. N. Rackham, P. Honey, M. Colbert, Wellens Publishing, Guilsborough, England.

Relationships (B)

The Sociogram is a very useful method of highlighting issues with individual relationships and different levels of contribution in working sets. The transactions which take place between individuals are recorded using the Sociogram Figure 1. The observer sits outside the set and writes the names of the participants normally going from left to right around the table. He then records each time one individual speaks to another on the appropriate line. In the example shown in figure 2 Derek has spoken eight times and has been spoken to eight times, he has spoken four times to John, once to Stephen and three times to Hilary. John has spoken nine times and received ten inputs. He has spoken four times to Derek, and five times to Hilary, but not at all to Stephen. Stephen has spoken six times and received two responses, once to John, twice to Derek and three times to Hilary. Hilary has spoken nine times and received eleven responses; three times to Derek, five times to John and once to Stephen.

It can be seen quite clearly from an analysis of this sociogram that Stephen is not really part of the conversation. He is trying to contribute but nobody seems to want to listen to him apart from Hilary who is probably just being sympathetic. This can now be fed back to the set and used to highlight Stephen's inability, for whatever reason, to make a meaningful contribution to the discussion.

SOCIOGRAM

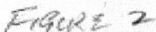

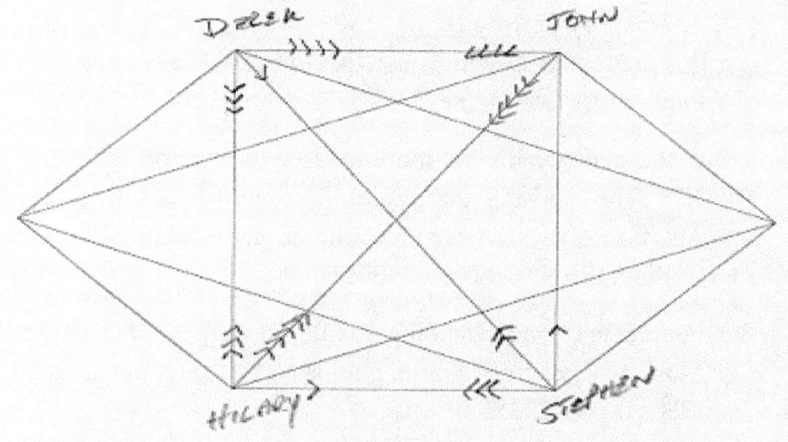

Further Reading

If you have found reading this book interesting you may also find the following useful.

1. For an insight into human behaviour I recommend Dr. Thomas A. Harris is the author of *I'm OK – You're OK*, the 1969 bestseller based upon the ideas of Transactional Analysis by <u>Dr Eric Berne</u>. ISBN 0-06-072427. If you find this interesting you may also like to read 'The Games People Play, by Dr Eric Berne ISBN 0-345-41003-3

2. In the same géndre but more focused on 'rapport' skills is NPL, How to Build a Successful Life by Richard Brandler, Alessio Roberti & Owen Fitzpatrick, published by Harper Collins, ISBN 978-0-00-749741-6

3. For a deeper understanding of values I suggest 'What Matters Most' by Hyrum W Smith, published by Franklin Covey Co. ISBN 0-684-87256-0

4. For an entertaining insight into the real world of influencing I recommend the book 'When I Stop Talking You'll Know I'm Dead by Jerry Weintraub, Rich Cohen and George Clooney, Published by Hachette Books ISBN 978-0-446-54815-1

5. To learn more about 'action learning' I recommend Reg's original book on the subject 'The ABC of Action Learning' Published by Gower Publications, ISBN 978-1-4094-2703-2. Mike Pedlar's Action Learning in Practice, Third Edition, Ed Mike Pedler, Gower Press, ISBN 0 566 07795 7 and More than Management Development, Edited by David Casey & David Pearce, Gower Press, 1977. ISBN 0-566-022005-X This book reviews the early GEC programmes referred to in this text.

6. If you would like to learn more about Facilitation then 'Facilitating Action Learning: A Practitioner's Guide' by <u>Mike Pedler</u> and <u>Christine Abbott</u> is a useful read. Also

David Casey's excellent paper on The Emerging Role of the Set Advisers, copies available from ALA International

Books George has written on Action Learning and related topics

The following books are published by ALA International. they are available on our web site www.ala-international.com and from **Google Books** and **Amazon** in Epub or paperback formats.

Books about Action learning

Applications of Action Learning – describes the philosophy of action learning and its applications. ISBN 978-0-9560822-4-4

Own Job Action Learning – describes how Action learning can be used in individual development programmes. ISBN 978-0-9560822-0-6

In-Plant Action Learning – explains how the philosophy of Action learning can be used to deliver organisational change. ISBN 978-0-9560822-3-7

In-Plant Action Learning Teams, Participants Guide – This Guide is designed to help In-Plant teams to self-manage and facilitate their own learning; available from ALA International.

Facilitated Learning – describes how the process of facilitation is used to develop participants in Action Learning sets. ISBN 978-0 - 9560822-9-9

Books about Personal Development

Managers as Leaders - This book show how management and leadership combine to ensure the effective delivery of the task. ISBN 978-0-9560822-2-0

Managing Difficult Relationships – examines the reasons for difficult relationships and provides a 'framework' for negotiating win / win solutions. ISBN 978-0-9560822-5-1

Change; Become a Winner - I believe that life is not a rehearsal, it's a journey and you can change it. If you would like to do something different with your life this book is for you. ISBN 13 978-1503185401, ISBN 10:1503185400

Books about Productivity

Values & Style; the Key to Productivity –The common denominator in performance improvement in organizations, is managing style. The things that stop people doing the best job they can stem from 'them and us' attitudes. These are based on cultural values and determine the way human beings perceive their roles and relationships within hierarchies. This book explores the nature of values and style and how they impact the operating effectiveness of organizations and societies.

Re-Engineering the Workplace – This book describes the Japanese approach to productivity with practical examples on how it can be applied in practice.

Useful web sites for Action Learning

Action Learning is a worldwide network. The following are some useful contacts in the Action Learning world:-

The International Foundation for Action Learning (IFAL), formally The Action Learning Trust www.ifal.org.uk

International Community of Action Learners (ICAL) This is a loose federation of Action Learning practitioners. Their web site can be found on www.tlainc.com

IMC acts as a clearing house for academic institutions offering Action Learning programmes. Contact www.imc.org.uk/imcal-inter For articles www.free-press.com/journals/gaja

The Revans Library at Salford University www.salford.ac.uk

World Institute for Action Learning, www.wial.com

Global Executive Learning – Formed in 1996 this international set focus on the use of Action Learning to deliver business solutions. http://www.global-executive-learning.com/index.php/en/2013-08-29-11-59-43/our-foundation

Please use the following link to find our books on Amazon.

http://www.amazon.com/s?ie=UTF8&page=1&rh=n%3A283155%2Cp_27%3AGeorge%20Boulden

I will be very grateful if you will take a few minutes to write a review on this book while you are there. Thank you.

George Boulden

www.ingramcontent.com/pod-product-compliance
Lightning Source LLC
Chambersburg PA
CBHW061445180526
45170CB00004B/1560

* 9 7 8 1 5 2 3 4 0 5 6 4 0 *